Grace and Fresh Ink:
52 Devotional Stories for the Seasons of Faith

Dedication

For David, the best husband on the planet. I am more grateful than I have words to express that you are the one I get to walk hand in hand with. You believe in me, always, hold tight when I slip, and challenge me with your amazing capacity to wildly follow the Creator. Thank-you!

For Meaghan, Hannah, Emily and Evan, who fill my world with extravagant love, laughter, and hope. Thank you for your beautiful, kind and encouraging words, and for your hearts that seek Grace.

Grace and Fresh Ink:
52 Devotional Stories for the Seasons of Faith

Katharine Barrett

Grace and Fresh Ink:
52 Devotional Stories for the Seasons of Faith
by Katharine Barrett

Copyright © 2012 by Katharine Barrett
All rights reserved.
This book or parts thereof may not be reproduced in any form, stored in a retrieval system or transmitted in any form by any means - electronic, mechanical, photocopy, recording, or otherwise - without the prior written permission of the publisher, except as provided by copyright law.

Published by Fresh Ink Media
ISBN: 978-0-9880768-0-8

Scripture marked **GW** is taken from **God's Word to the Nations**. Copyright 1995 by Baker Publishing Group. Used by permission. All rights reserved.

Scripture marked **NASB** is taken from the **NEW AMERICAN STANDARD BIBLE**. Copyright The Lockman Foundation 1960, 1962, 1963, 1968, 1971, 1972 1973, 1975, 1977, 1995. Used by permission.

Scripture marked **NCV** is taken from the **New Century Version**. Copyright 2005 by Thomas Nelson Inc. Used by permission. All rights reserved.

Scripture marked **MSG** is taken from **The Message**. Copyright 1993 by NavPress Publishing Group. Used by permission.

Scripture marked **GNT** is taken from the **Good News Bible, Today's English Version**. Copyright American Bible Society 1966, 1971, 1976, 1992. Used by permission.

Scripture marked **NIV** is taken from the **HOLY BIBLE, NEW INTERNATIONAL VERSION. NIV**. Copyright 1973, 1978, 1984 by International Bible Society. Used by permission of Zondervan. All rights reserved.

Scripture marked **NLT** is taken from the **Holy Bible, New Living Translation**. Copyright 1996 by Tyndale House Publishers, Inc. Wheaton, IL 60189. Used by permission. All rights reserved.

Scripture marked **KJV** is taken from the **King James Version of the Bible**. (Public Domain.)

Cover Design by Katharine Barrett
Cover and interior photographs copyright 2012 by Katharine Barrett

"Be who you are and say what you feel because those who mind don't matter and those who matter don't mind."

-Dr. Seuss

GRACE AND FRESH INK

TABLE OF CONTENTS

~ INTRODUCTION ~	1
SPRING	3
Loud	4
A Time to Plant	6
Thankful for Grace	8
I Went Walking	10
Flying a Flag	12
Walking and Fighting	14
Outside the Lines	17
Why Easter?	19
On Being a Mom	21
In the Becoming	24
Holding My Breath	26
Shade Gardens	29
Color Me Loved	31

GRACE AND FRESH INK

SUMMER	**35**
Storm	36
Blooming Hydrangeas	38
Rusty Metal	41
Travelling with Baggage	44
Thirsty	47
A Royal Story	49
Complicated	51
Chipped and Cracked	53
Shall We Dance?	55
Rain	57
Kitchen Talk	59
What Are You Called?	61
The Swing at Dusk	64
AUTUMN	67
For Tomorrow	68

Authentic	70
It's a Tree!	73
It's in the Everyday	75
Forever and Always	77
Why?	80
Autumn Reflections	84
Always Remember	86
Sometimes and Always	88
Walking with Angels	90
Lifting My Head	94
Daughters	96
Grapes and Grace	98
WINTER	101
A Cup of Quiet	102
Letting in the Light	104
Drumming and Belonging	106

I Get It!	**108**
Weary	**110**
What's on Your List?	**112**
The Big Picture	**114**
Hark the Herald Angels	**116**
The Stone of Help	**118**
A New Year	**120**
Otters and Love	**123**
Beautiful Refuge	**126**
Waiting for Spring	**128**
~ ABOUT THE AUTHOR ~	**133**

~ Introduction ~

G*race*. It's in the everyday. In real life. It is under the laundry pile, and behind the desk. It's there in our sun filled days, dark sleepless nights and all of our beautiful mess. It covers us. It swirls around us, and whispers for us to stop, see, and know it. When we do, we find gratitude spilling out around us, fresh ink on the pages of our lives.

Grace. It flows unbounded through our seasons and days and its source is Love. Indescribable, unconditional, beautiful: Love. And it's writing our story! Lines, paragraphs and chapters, woven together with His story. He knows each of the times when we've picked up the pen and tried to write it ourselves. He was there when water rushed unbridled from broken places, making the writing illegible. He's good with all of the wrinkled pages, coffee stained corners, and worn edges.

So let's be honest. When we share our stories, honestly, and authentically, we empower each other. We give each other tools that point us

GRACE AND FRESH INK

toward hope and healing. More importantly, we give and receive Grace. And it's beautiful!

There is power in story; yours, mine, His. The best part? It's not finished! There are blank pages still waiting for fresh ink. This is an amazing journey we are travelling. Each footstep echoes the presence of Grace and the chance for gratitude, as we sift through pages and paragraphs and allow the God of the universe to write the story!

SPRING

Loud

I am distracted. The bedroom door, without warning, slams shut. Twice I've heard the swishing of fabric and thought for sure that someone was walking past the living room. Thinking that the TV has been left on, I reach for the remote, only to see a dark screen. I jump at the unusual noises, the loudness.

Then I remember.

Stiff winds shut bedroom doors.

A baby's cry, and tires squealing on the pavement.

The scuffling of squirrels on the rough bark of the plum tree.

Fresh breezes blow the curtains at the window.

Walkers in pairs loudly discuss the day.

It is Spring, and I have opened all the windows, filling the rooms with fresh, clean, crisp and new.

Winter's silence is over.

Spring is beautiful and loud.

Look! The winter is past, the rain is over and gone. Blossoms appear in the land. The time of the songbird has arrived. Song of Solomon 2:11,12 (GW)

A Time to Plant

He digs his small chubby fingers into warm soil, and I smile. The breeze plays in his soft curls and side by side we plant seeds. He hums unknown notes, rivaling the song of the birds who study us from the fence top. Sweat trickles down back and brow as the sun stands behind us, lighting up our work, our world.

I tell him what is weed and what is good. I show him how to make a hole with a thumb, and watch while the seeds drop into crooked rows. There is a contented feeling of being. Just being. Questions spill out on the fragrant earth. Slow at first and then faster. I run to catch up with answers. Why do we hide seeds? What makes them grow? How do they know when to come out? Do we need water? Will it happen soon? Eyes wide and hands dirty, he waits for the replies.

We look at small green shoots, already up more than an inch, and I remind him that they are answering a call. God created them, and He tells them when to grow and bloom. Yes, the same God who made the dog, and the rain. I clasp warm muddy fingers in mine, and I tell him again how very much God loves all that he created, especially him. Grace and gratitude spill out on topsoil as he and I discuss in the simplest of ways that the life in the seeds is like God's life in him. He smiles at the thought and I whisper how excited I am about his growing and becoming.

It's no longer just my garden, it's holy ground. We pat the earth firm and watch a stream of water soak down to thirsty seeds. The fence creates a backdrop for our shadows. I smile at the wonder of a small son brushing warm soil from chubby fingers. Side by side we survey our work.

Seeds have been planted. Beautiful, sacred, crooked rows. Seeds of hope, faith, and love. Watered by everyday Grace.

Thankful for Grace

It has been a very long day. I wish I could say that all the choices I made today were good ones. I want to believe that this cloak of tiredness that envelopes me was the result of a day well spent. But I can't.

Somewhere in the fog of weary sadness, I know it's because I argued when I should have kept silent, stood in the forefront of demand when I should have stepped aside. All my thoughts on listening well, float just out of reach and taunt me. I jumped in with both feet, half listening, letting annoyance plug my ears.

I wasn't wrong, but I wasn't right either.

It was a day full of sudden changes, schedules, disappointments, busyness, and frustration. Lots of reasons to provide excuse, none of which will actually come forward to take the blame.

The tangled web of actions, reactions, angry words, missteps, regret, and frustration cling to me like a damp sweater on a rainy evening. I cannot start over, change the day, or my reaction to it. It's not possible to call back words or undo actions. There are no tools for rolling back time, no exchange or refund for things that did not turn out as I expected.

There is one thing I can do. I go to the One who understands me. At His cross, I leave the soggy sweater. He wraps me in the warmth of His Forgiveness and I touch Grace. In His arms I am reminded that I belong, and in His hands He holds a clean white shawl. It is light, exquisite and unmarred. I hear Him say, "For tomorrow."

I will sleep with Grace as the softest of pillows, and with Love wrapped around me like a quilt. I know that new mercy will come with the morning and with every breath that closes the gap between the day and night, I am thankful.

The LORD'S loving kindnesses indeed never cease, for His compassions never fail. They are new every morning; Great is Your faithfulness. Lamentations 3:22, 23 (NASB)

I Went Walking

I went walking today, with an inquisitive four year old. He stopped to look at things I take for granted, and delighted in simple questions and answers. We found new growth on tree branches.
What is this?
The little hard things? Those are casings (actually scales, I've since found out.) They protect the buds 'til it's time for the blooms and leaves to come out.
Oh.
God planned it that way so they would be protected.
God made it that way?
Yep.
When I got home, I went for a walk with the God of the universe. He delights in showing me the things I take for granted and answering my questions.
So, if you are protecting the buds on the trees, are you protecting me, my heart?
Yes, that's what I want to do.
So what is it that I have already wrapped around

myself, my heart?
Self-protection.
Oh.

I love you. I am your shelter, your refuge, your protector. I planned it that way, so that in the right time you will bloom!

I will say to the Lord, "You are my place of safety and protection. You are my God and I trust you." Psalm 91.2 (NCV)

Flying a Flag

Every month or so, I change the flag that waves from the pole, on our front porch post. It is the only flag on the street! Flags just aren't as popular here, as they are in the US. It is on our trips south to visit family that I purchase them so that I have a variety to choose from. The kids get a chuckle out of my "drawer FULL of flags"

Our neighbors have come to expect the changes, and if I have one up past its prime, the nice man 4 doors down will comment as he walks his dog, "Morning! When do we get to see the next flag?" It's become a marker. When our kids give directions to the house, they say, "It's the house with the flag."

I love how the flags catch the light, radiating warmth and welcome, even when it's bitterly cold. They are distinctive, and beautiful, and I love watching them wave in the breeze! They usually convey a message. "Welcome"   "Happy Easter" "Autumn Blessings"   "Welcome to the Nut

House" (no, we don't have that one, but there are days when it would be totally appropriate).

I thought about living a life like this, when I was admiring the flag this morning. To be distinctive and beautiful. Living lives that convey a message of encouragement, humor, love and blessing. Always changing, but remaining a steady marker and direction point. A catch and release, of the amazing light that comes from the God of the universe. Radiating, warm, and welcoming, no matter who walks by, or what the season.

Here's another way to put it: You're here to be light, bringing out the God-colors in the world. God is not a secret to be kept. We're going public with this, as public as a city on a hill. If I make you light-bearers, you don't think I'm going to hide you under a bucket, do you? I'm putting you on a light stand. Now that I've put you there on a hilltop, on a light stand—shine! Keep open house; be generous with your lives. By opening up to others, you'll prompt people to open up with God, this generous Father in heaven. Matthew 5:14-16 (MSG)

Walking and Fighting

Have you ever done something, and afterwards wondered why you'd never done it before? A friend and I decided to get our exercise (not just meandering) by walking one morning - early.

On the evening before, I e-mailed her this question:

"What if it's raining?"

She replied, "Bring an umbrella!" (cue eye rolling and a deep sigh)

When I left home (bleary eyed and wondering what I'd gotten myself into) the air was clear and it looked like it was going to be a nice day. I arrived at her house (seriously, only five minutes down the road) and dark clouds rolled in; the wind was picking up! As we started walking, the heavens opened and it poured. It rained for most of the walk. It was great (although I had muscles voicing complaints the next day!)

When I got home, my husband mentioned that he didn't think we'd go. I almost always say no, to doing things in the rain! I'm not sure why. I remember when I was in college and my husband and I would walk and ride in any weather (I would have braved anything to spend time with him!) Somewhere in the years that followed, I convinced myself that it was safer to stay in. It sounds so silly, and yet when I was walking I just kept thinking - why have I never done this before?

Why have I let the rain stop me? I wonder what else I don't do because it's comfortable, safe, or I believe the little voice that says I can't, or shouldn't. And, how often do I let pride dictate what I do (what if I'm seen dripping wet at 6 am?) When I say it out loud, some of it is laughable, and yet I think these things really do keep us captive! I want to run this part of the race, and finish well. Yesterday, I started by taking back rainy days. I will walk no matter what the weather! I am ready to fight, and even more so after reading this...

The weapons we use in our fight are not the world's weapons but God's powerful weapons, which we use to destroy strongholds. We destroy false arguments; we pull down every proud obstacle that is raised against the knowledge of God; we take every thought captive and make it obey Christ. 2 Corinthians 10:4-5 (GNT)

Yesterday, my weapon of choice was truth! I never thought of myself as a fighter, but I'm pretty sure when I picked up the tools He's given me, I heard my Heavenly Father say... way to go girl, let's do this! What about you? Do you have things that stop you? What God tools are you using?

Outside the Lines

They said to stay inside the lines. And so, with unsteady, primary fingers she forced the color inside the lines. Praise was the result of the effort. "It's perfect," they said! And ever after, she never colored outside the lines. Early lessons are the ones best learned: When things are perfect, everyone is happy. The other side of the much tarnished coin is this: You cannot be happy unless everything is perfect.

Nothing is ever perfect.

Life is messy, hard, unfair, and difficult to understand. But somehow, those of us who have believed that life must be lived in this state of perfection try to make it happen. We try so hard. And while we're doing it, we fail to realize that it is not living. It is existing. We put off living while we focus on how to make it perfect, but it is not our job to make it perfect. It never was.

Life is not perfect, but God is Good. Always. And He is life. When we wait for life to be perfect, we miss the chance to bless the good. To focus on the love of the creator of the universe, that is all around us. Those moments of giving thanks, to Him and for Him. Thankful for everything that's come from Him...out of love.

Love doesn't make us stay inside the lines. He's always there in the middle of the mess, and pain, and imperfection. Love knows no fear. He's not worried about the stuff I cannot change or fix. He says we'll work on that together. When we know the safety of true redemptive love, we can shift our focus, and begin to discover grace, gratitude and hope. Where there is hope, there is freedom. Freedom to take the hand of God and run, dance, and discover. Freedom to sit quietly, listen, give thanks and smile: And to color outside the lines.

Why Easter?

I breathe in the comforting smell of dirt, rain, and new grass. I close my eyes, listening to the wind blowing wild in the pine trees. I squeeze the soft, strong hand of the best husband, and I whisper, "Easter's coming." Of all the holidays, this one is my favourite.

It's not predictable.

We have hunted for eggs in the heat of a sun that rivalled a mid-July day. Winter coats have protected us when snowflakes swirled, as the sun broke the horizon on Easter Sunday.

It's often underplayed, and overlooked. The white flowers have bloomed on the plant, whose name I can't remember. Everything is pregnant with life, hope. We struggle from winter's enveloping sleep, and if we are not intentional, we'll miss it. We use the longer days to quicken our step and crowd the obvious with the urgent. Spring reminds us to lift our heads and journey to Easter.

From death to life. A constant communion, nature calling us to remember! The daffodils nod their heads in affirmation. On Good Friday we will walk with others who want to remember, to sit in sorrow so that we can rejoice in new life!

It calls us to reflect. Mixing up spices for bread, I will contemplate the women before me who gathered spices for a tomb. We will keep company with friends and those we love. Eating, laughing, loving. And like the company before us, we will recite for our children, our hearts, why it is that we do this.

It calls us into Love. I scuff the stones on the driveway, and I breathe love. Love that lived and died and moved a stone for me. Love that wraps around me tight, no matter what. Always. Love that lives in me. Amazing, Infinite, Love.

In remembrance, at Easter.

On Being a Mom

She asked me, just on the spur of the moment, what I thought. What was the most important thing a mother could do or be for her child? The room of busy, chatting people seemed to grow silent. What was the answer?

Mothers. Card stores are filled with aisle-long racks full of cards that try to express the feelings we have when it comes to Mom. Laughter, Gratefulness, Thanks, Admiration, Friendship and Love. The relationship we have with our mothers can be the longest relationship we have with anyone in our lives. Four of the greatest moments in my life have been in a hospital bed, welcoming our children into the world. It is an amazing, wonderful, joyful gift to be their Mom!

Our household of six often means lots of noise. Part of that noise is lots of laughter. It means a minimum of 12 pairs of shoes in our front hall, most of them having already tracked something through the kitchen. It means pushing a large cart full of groceries every two weeks, and more laundry than I ever could have imagined when we looked at each other and said "let's have four kids!"

It means four different personalities, different needs. It means endless questions and honest admissions to not always having the answers. It's a full time, 24 hour, on call job, and I would be lying to you if I didn't say that it is often frustrating, and exhausting. I think it was the Christmas that we all had the stomach flu at the same time when I realized we'd never be able to do a Hallmark commercial! It means quiet moments, giggles, and busy days danced to the music of sweet words and sticky fingers.

My children's dependence on me has been a constant reminder of my dependence on God. The phrases "living out loud" and "love in action" take on a new meaning in the light of four pair of observing eyes.

Being Mom is a learning process. I have learned that while I am straightening up those piles of shoes, I have the opportunity to pray for the owners of each pair. Good communication and time spent together are important and non-negotiable, and in the light of eternity, it's just a load of laundry. It's a moment by moment walk, leaving footprints that surprise us. Life twists and turns, we learn from each other and there is Grace in all of it. Children are an incredible gift from God. Being their mom is a privilege.

The answer to the question? I believe, the best thing a mother can do for her children, is to know, and experience how much she is loved by the God of the universe. When we live loved, it changes everything. Including, being a Mom.

In the Becoming

The other night, just as it was getting dark, I was walking outside along the side of the house. Our lovely neighbors have a beautiful "green fence." It consists of vines, plants and trees that provide a wonderful, green privacy fence, between our properties. Some of the plants were beginning to flower and bud, and I wanted to take a closer look. I discovered odd, misshapen little green lumps on the ends of the stems.

One of these days they will be luscious berries! Lots and lots of them! They looked a little awkward (and complex) and gnarly at that moment, but I knew they would look amazing when it was time! Now, the question was... black berries or raspberries? I wasn't sure. I just didn't know enough about them...although I was leaning towards raspberries. Next time I see our neighbor, I will have to ask.

Before the light completely faded, I grabbed my camera. I wanted to remember the berries this way, before they ripen. I wanted a reminder that sometimes, even with amazing, created life inside, we can look awkward and gnarly. I am too quick to judge the awkward, in others and in myself. What I was created to be may be a bit hazy to me at times, but not to the God of the universe. He knows what He created, knows what it will look like, and He is head over heels delighted, from flower to fruit and with every gnarly bit in between! We are loved, and He knows what He's doing!

I praise you because you made me in an amazing and wonderful way. What you have done is wonderful. I know this very well. Psalm 139:14 (NCV)

I am thankful for His life in me, for His thoughts of Love and creative amazing plans! And I'm thankful for berries in the light of dusk.

Holding My Breath

It's a fact. Something that is. Like air. We are loved. Unconditionally and forever.

There is nothing we can do to make God love us more.

I know we want to believe it, but so much of our lives we have believed the opposite. And so we hold our breath, and repeat the list. You know, that list in your head that gets repeated, when you think about God's love:

Be good
Serve others
Strive to be perfect
Get involved
Read
Study
Pray
Be kind
Have it all together

Now before you fill my inbox with protests, hear me out. We are talking about love here.

*There is nothing we can do
to make God love us less.*

Not even the things we hide, those places inside that we alone know about, the ones we lock tight:
Anger
Secrets
Impatience
Un-forgiveness
Indifference
Hatred
Lies
Control

This is not about what we do, or don't do. This is about who He is.

He is love

All He asks is that we let Him love us. Let go, and jump into the vast expanse of His love. He knows all of our lists. He knows all about the things we fear will keep Him from loving us. And He's OK with all of it.

O Lord, you have examined me, and you know me. You alone know when I sit down and when I get up. You read my thoughts from far away. You watch me when I travel and when I rest. You are familiar with all my ways. Psalm 139:1-3 (GW)

When we begin to accept that amazing love then the things we do are in response to His love, not a means to procure it. We don't live in the fear of what we've done wrong, because He will help us open up all those locked places, and His love will free us.

Where can I go to get away from your Spirit? Where can I run to get away from you? ...If I say, "Let the darkness hide me and let the light around me turn into night," even the darkness is not too dark for you. Night is as bright as day. Darkness and light are the same to you. Psalm 139:7,11,12 (GW)

He loves us, and it is not because He has to. We are His creation. We belong to Him. It's that love that draws us into a relationship that is pure and true, and there is nowhere else we want to be!

So jump, and exhale, because...When we live loved... we can breathe!

Shade Gardens

While I readily confess that I need the sun and light, I am also a big fan of the shade. A few years ago, a friend offered me some plants from her garden. She was dividing them, and they were of the shade-loving variety. I never say no to greenery! There were three types, and after a bit of preparation, they found a new home under my evergreens in a shady corner of our back yard. They grew well, produced small white and purple flowers, variegated leaves and they're hardy! They survived my husband mistakenly dumping soil on them in late Fall, and they survived our winter snows. Even a new puppy couldn't beat them!

While I was clearing away dead leaves and leftover fall debris from around the quickly growing shoots, I was thinking about my friend. She is a lot like the shade garden she has helped me to produce. She is happy not to be in the forefront, allowing others to soak up the full light of the sun. But she does bloom. If you are close enough, the flowers will catch your eye, not large and showy like my Hydrangeas or Roses, just quiet and simple like the tiny white blossoms on the Sweet Woodruff. She is hardy and strong. She has survived Cancer, and conquered things that no one thought she could. The plants in my garden are the spreading kind. They reach to cover the ground around my trees. My friend has stretched her compassion to reach beyond this continent and works to help children she has never met, in countries across the sea.

When I look out my window at my little shade garden, I am reminded of my friend. I'm thankful for her generosity both in my shade loving plants and in my life. I am thankful for my Heavenly Father, who has blessed me with a garden of friends of all different types. He knows and chooses what I need to bloom alongside me in this life.

Whether you are a sun-drenched flower or a shade loving one, I hope your day is full of the blessing of a well-watered garden. Tended and cared for with Love, by the God of the universe.

Color Me Loved

I love paint swatches. Maybe it's the scope of possibility, or reason to dream. It may be as simple as a love of color and all the exotic names. Whatever the reason, I enjoy browsing the hardware stores multi-colored cards, while my husband ponders lengths of rope or lumber. Imagine how thrilled I was, when a small carport addition called for new paint!

I knew just what I wanted, or at least what I thought I wanted. I asked for opinions. I patiently painted squares of color from sample pots to try and envision the rooms after they had been bathed in my choice. It was almost unanimous... my choice was too dark. What? They couldn't be right. I loved this color, it made my heart sing. It was warm and inviting.

Sometimes, the most beautiful choice isn't the right one.

There are times to forge ahead, and there are times to stand quietly and really listen. I stood in the middle of the echoing room and tried to listen.

GRACE AND FRESH INK

The first voice I heard was the accusing cry of a lie. That lie of "not good enough" that says I shouldn't be the one to choose in the first place. The lie that taunts, with past mistakes. The echo of the inferior was loud. I picked up a brush and began to paint another square.

I added the sound of my voice to the echoing room.

"It's just a paint color."

The next sound was my own laughter. Talking to thin air about paint may be a bigger problem than the color of the walls! My spirit hears the question: "What is the truth?" Under the skylight, with sunlight and birdsong as my accompaniment, I answered:

"Father, the truth is; this is just a paint color. Right or wrong, it doesn't define me. This need for approval slipped in and snatched away joy before I barely had time to stop it. The truth is that you don't keep track of mistakes. You believe in me, and you love it when I am "over the moon" about a paint color. It's part of the way you created me. The truth is, in your love there is no condemnation, no inferiority, only belonging."

A new sound entered, drowning out the rest. It's the truth of living loved. Standing in the security of Him I surveyed the wall and realized this: They were right. It will be too dark.

Grace filled the room. I gave thanks for their authentic, honest hearts. My brush began another square. "Saffron Strands" caught the afternoon sun, and I smiled at the warm glow. This might be it. This just may be the color, of living loved.

GRACE AND FRESH INK

SUMMER

Storm

The breeze called first in urgent tones,
and whispered in the pines.
It made the starlings take to flight,
and boxwoods start to sigh.

It swept a cloak of grey and black,
across the bits of blue,
And all that had been clear and bright,
was hidden from my view.

I laid aside my gloves and trowel,
as drums began to beat,
I watched a new insistent wind,
rush dry leaves down the street.

She finally arrived herself,
exciting, wild and free.
I waited while she passed the gate,
and then confronted me.

Water runs in rivulets, down cheeks
and off my nose.
The starling shakes his feathers dry,
chirping out his woes.
She left us all quite suddenly,
beautiful and warm;
The flurry of excitement,
that is the Summer storm.

Blooming Hydrangeas

My favorite flower is going to bloom! The Hydrangeas have buds! I didn't expect them to bloom this year... at all! I have three hydrangea bushes in my front garden. Every year they bloom in gorgeous shades of pink, blue, and lavender. Last year they were looking a little tired. The nice man at the nursery said I should cut them back, something I had never done. He said it may take a year for them to bloom again, and there was a chance they would stop blooming for a few years. If I didn't do anything they would become too tired and stop blooming and growing all together.

So when the weather got cool, I took my shears and cut back all the dead wood and then some. And I have been waiting for buds... they're usually starting to appear by mid- May, but there weren't any. Until last night. While I was sweeping the dust of the day off the porch, I saw tiny little green buds that had started to emerge.

Those little tiny buds will soon be beautiful blooms! They made it! Every one of them should be named Hope! They made it through my pruning, and our snowy winter. They hung on through the ice storms and the unusually cold spring. I'm sure it was a shock to go from cold to blistering hot almost overnight, but there are buds, in spite of, or because of it all. I'm guessing it's because there is life inside of them, always, no matter what it looks like. Life was put there by the Creator of the universe.

This morning, as I gazed over the porch rail to say good morning, I pondered this fact: His life is also in me, always, no matter what it looks like. Despite the pruning and the winters and the shocks (all the things I think I could really do without!) there will be growth and life and blooming, probably when I least expect it. There is always good and beautiful, because He is good... always.

I often admit to feeling tired. Some years have felt like a conveyor belt of one thing right after another. The kind of stuff that makes you want to yell, "Enough with the pruning shears already!" But those tiny little buds were a gentle reminder to hang in there, remembering who holds my life and all the seasons. Their tiny petals hold all the Hope of the God of the universe, who called them to bloom, and who speaks wonderful things into our lives!

Blessed are those whose help is the God of Jacob, whose hope is in the LORD their God. Psalm 146:5 (NIV)

Rusty Metal

In several "All about me" paragraphs, and sometimes in conversation, my love of rusty metal comes up. I think rusty metal is beautiful. I have often been drooling over a piece in a country store, only to hear my wonderful husband say "Don't we have one of those at home... without the rust? I could put it out in the rain for you!" I laugh, but the fact remains that I love the look of rusted metal! It is displayed prominently in my house, and not discarded or ignored...

Every year, I get things ready for my "Happy Place"(cue angelic choir). For a few brief and magnificent months, our covered front porch is a wonderful place to read, listen to birds, enjoy the flowers and blissfully revel in the quiet and warm weather. I spend as many moments as I can enjoying it, and I have lovely rusty wind chimes and decorations that I hang. They remind me of something amazing.

Rusty metal is not for everyone. It is often discarded, because for some there is no beauty in it. It is used, corroded, and when you handle it, it leaves messy orange/brown dust on your hands! While some pieces are rusted on purpose (to sell to people like me) most are in a rusty state due to neglect, mistreatment or misunderstanding. I buy them knowing that under the rust, is rust. I love it, just the way it is. I use it just the way it is, and it brings beauty and grace to our home. I know how to display it, where to place it so it will shine (yes, shine.)

Now here is the amazing part. The world is full of rusty metal people and I am one of them. Neglect, mistreatment, and the plain old rain of life have left us rusty, and maybe a bit messy. By the standards that exist in the world...we definitely don't have it as all together as the painted and polished (who, by the way, are rust hiding beneath a coat of paint)

Often, we take on the labels: discarded, ignored, or not quite good enough, but we are loved. Infinitely more than any of the pieces I own, the God of the universe loves rusty metal people, just the way we are. There is nothing I can do to make Him love me more, and nothing I can do will make Him love me less. He sees beauty when He looks at me. I am more than good enough, I am His. He wants to remove the lies and labels and is excited for me to be what He created me to be. And He will shine through me! So today, I will trust the God of the universe with me as I am, (He knows all of me anyway) and walk in the freedom of living loved!

Travelling with Baggage

Although I don't often have the chance, I love to travel. When I was 16, I went on my first trip to England, and fell in love with planes, trains and anything that would take me to a new destination! I love new places, cultures and the fun that comes with exploring and discovering them!

One year, during the months before we moved house, I had been organizing and purging, and finding a lot of things that I had gathered on my travels. You know the stuff you pick up? Little souvenirs that you think you need, and brochures, lots of them! The leaflets they give you when you walk into a gallery, museum or church. The ones you accept with a smile, even though you don't want or need one. Flyers, announcing events in the current town. Events I never went to. I've kept ticket stubs, rail passes, and even (horror) several gum wrappers! Until I opened a few boxes, I didn't even realize I still had all this stuff and I can't remember why so much of it was important enough to hold onto.

I have been thinking about the other things in life that I hold onto. This journey of life takes us to a lot of places, and we have picked up a lot of baggage. Not tangible stuff, but plenty of things we think we need. Souvenirs of security, to prove we're good enough, and the boxes of guilt that come with it, to remind us that even with them, we still don't measure up. "Brochures" of shame. Some we picked up on our own, some were handed to us, and we took them without question. Expectations! The ones we have had for ourselves, and all the ones we let others put on us. Souvenirs of fear, guilt, shame, insecurity, expectations and other things we don't realize we're carrying. And if we do, we also carry the lie that says we have to hang on to them.

This is the best part of this journey story. We can let someone start sorting the boxes, and getting rid of the stuff. The God of the universe is so good at opening boxes, letting in light and truth and helping to pry our fingers from all the baggage we've been carrying. It is difficult to be what you were created to be, weighted down with "stuff". He replaces all the baggage with truth, and I never imagined travelling light could feel this amazing, wonderful and free!

GRACE AND FRESH INK

Not all the stuff we gather needs to be let go of. I have a beautiful wood carving from a trip I took to Ireland. I remember the time and place that I purchased it and it is a wonderful memory! This is part of the good "stuff". The things I am thankful for and bless. Just in case you think I live in a perfect, all-together, (cue angelic choir) life; these travelling thoughts were born during a season of getting-ready-to-sell-a-house-chaos. There was an emotional box. Unopened. It had been sitting completely undetected, until the lid blew off. Not all the contents were pretty. I asked the Lord to begin sorting, He does it so gently, and completely. In the end, there is always light and truth!

So if the Son sets you free, you will be free indeed. John 8:36 (NIV)

Thirsty

My good coffee in a great mug is hot and strong. I have been sitting here for a long time. I have been staring at an empty screen and letting the quiet of the morning sink in. Rain is dripping slowly down the window to my right, and it is so needed.

It will not be enough though. It is a light shower, which will be good, but we haven't had rain in quite a while. We need a good long, soaking rain. The kind that gets deep down into the soil, nourishing the roots. We need water that will keep my beautiful hydrangeas from wilting when the heat comes in waves.

I sometimes feel like my back garden plants. Moments, days and weeks, are busy. Life spins at an often dizzying pace, with few breaks. In the busy rush of the good and necessary, I have only allowed my spirit a sprinkling shower. You know that feeling? When I stop long enough to listen, I hear the refrain of self-sufficiency. I've managed things quite well on my own (thank you very much), and depended on myself. Now, there are roots drying out. There hasn't been rain, the deep down nourishing rain that the God of the universe is so good and willing to pour out on my spirit. The kind that keeps me hydrated when things get hot. It is life giving and refreshing and I am thirsty!

   I know that letting go and trusting Him again with everything, will open up the heavens. I will be flooded again, and He is good, always. I don't want to be content with light showers. That's existing, and I am not content to exist. I don't want to settle for anything less than this: To spend my moments and days experiencing crazy, unconditional, beautiful, all encompassing Love. The love of the Spirit who breathes Life into me, and who floods my soul.

For I will pour water on the thirsty land, and streams on the dry ground; I will pour out my Spirit on your offspring, and my blessing on your descendants. Isaiah 44:3 (NIV)

A Royal Story

Sometimes it seems as if the world has Royal fever! Everywhere we turn these days there is something being said, written, or photographed in connection with England's royal family. Leading up to the wedding of William and Kate, it was even more intense. I didn't follow the news too closely, but my youngest daughter did. I remember how she feels. I can't believe it was thirty years ago (yikes) when I kept a scrapbook, collected memorabilia, and got up in the early hours of the morning to watch Charles and Diana's fairy tale wedding.

There was just something about the story. A real-life version of the stories we'd read before bed since we were little. A prince, a princess, a beautiful gown, a fabulous church and a horse drawn carriage. It was all just perfect for the hopeless romantics (yes, me.)

Of course there was the rest of the story. We grew up and so did they. The fairy tale fell apart in front of the world and ended in tragedy. And now, there is another story.

GRACE AND FRESH INK

What is it about royalty that fascinates us? Charles and Diana's wedding was viewed by a global audience (somewhere around 750 million) and they estimated that the audience for William's wedding was even greater! Maybe it is the feeling of being able to witness history in the making. Hundreds of years from now, other generations will read the account of the wedding and its effect on the world and the royal line.

There is one more Royal story...mine. I am part of a Royal family.

My Father is the King above all other Kings, the God of the universe. I am a daughter of the King, with all the right, authority, privilege, and inheritance that come with His name. Yes, that makes me a princess! It is an amazing story of sacrifice, and belonging. My life carries the seal of His house. It's an on-going, real-life story of Love, hope, redemption, healing and Grace!

In all the craziness of royal reporting, I am glad for the reminder of whom I belong to and who writes my royal story. I hope your day is full of beautiful stories and a heart full of belonging!

The Spirit you received does not make you slaves, so that you live in fear again; rather, the Spirit you received brought about your adoption to sonship. And by him we cry, "Abba, Father." Romans 8:15 (NIV)

Complicated

One Monday morning, just as I was about to empty my heart and head by way of my clicking keyboard keys, the computer began malfunctioning. I've learned enough to explore and fix a lot of problems, but not this time. As I was shutting it down, one of our children announced that the air conditioning in our van had stopped functioning. There was nothing I could do to fix that except confirm the diagnosis. And so Monday rolled into Tuesday, with a chain of things, most complicated and urgent, trailing behind me. It seems as though when one thing is attended to, another attaches itself to the end. The chain gets longer, and so does the overwhelming feeling that I am getting nowhere.

Sometimes when things are most complicated, it is best to return to the simple. Picking up the tools I have come to love, I head to the yard. I am reminded while I am surveying the garden, and plunging my fingers into warm, fragrant earth, that this is how it was meant to be.

Life. Created life. Nurtured, tended and blossoming into what it was meant to be. Beautiful, fruitful...

While I plan and plant, the stress of the complicated washes into the street with the water from my hose. I wish for it to always feel like this. No stress or strain. Nothing malfunctioned, broken, dysfunctional. But that is not real or honest.

This is earth. We live in the messy, the complicated, the strain of everyday, and the raw of the fallen. So what should it look like then, living here, longing for there, with a Spirit full of created life?

I stop to look at the chain behind me. I am holding on. I can begin by letting go of the links that I cannot fix, and allowing the God of the universe to take them. I can start by asking for forgiveness, and choosing to forgive. I seem to constantly forget that I am not in charge of all of this. So kneeling in the dirt, I spread my hands and offer up control. He is here. Loving me. In all of it. In the messy, complicated, daily life. And all of it becomes Holy.

Because the one who is in you is greater than the one who is in the world. 1 John 4.4 (NIV)

Chipped and Cracked

I saw it again. I was looking for vases to hold some of the beautiful summer blooms that are appearing in the garden. Quite a few years ago we were helping my parents sift through the contents of their house in preparation for their move to an apartment. A number of things had to be given away or sold in the process of downsizing.

One afternoon I was going through a box of things that had been labeled "Good Will" and I came across a small glass pitcher. I remembered that it had belonged to my grandmother, and I have a clear memory of my mother putting cereal cream in it for my grandfather. When I asked why it was in the box, my mother pointed to a large chip on the edge of the spout. "It can't be used anymore."

"I'll take it," I said quickly, as if there were a dozen others wanting it! My sister glanced at the box of things I had already claimed and asked, "What are you going to do with it?" Good question. What was I going to do with it? I wasn't sure, but it was a connection to my grandmother, someone I had never known except through stories. And so I put it in my box.

That summer, I took out the pitcher, and filled it with small roses from our back garden. It makes a wonderful vase! The "chip" doesn't matter. In fact, it has become part of the story, and it is beautiful.

It is a small glass reminder of Mercy and Grace. When we come to the God of the Universe, we aren't discarded because of "chips and cracks". Life is full of "counter high drops onto tile floor" kind of situations! He has a purpose. He knows our story, and He's good with it. All of it! He sees His Son in us, and says that we are beautiful, amazing, and altogether lovely! He puts His life in us, and we display His Mercy, Grace and Love.

If you find yourself in the "chipped and cracked" category, Welcome! You are in good company. We are deeply loved and never discarded! Join me in celebrating Grace, belonging, and a whole lot of blooming Love!

Shall We Dance?

Sometimes I have such a full heart and spirit that I am afraid to open the door and let out the words. Afraid that they will spill out around me like unruly raindrops on the driveway, big, sloppy and random, leaving nothing but a murky mess. Sometimes, a mess can be beautiful...
In the stillness of the morning I let the full weight of thoughts tumble out on the faded carpet.
Me.
He loves Me.
Loved Me, before even the first flash of my creation took place.
Knew me, wanted me, designed me.

Me.
Weighted down with cumbersome bags of heartbreak, abuse, pain, hurt, disorders, denial.
He loves Me. He comes.
He offers to take the bags.

Me.

GRACE AND FRESH INK

Caked with mud in layers of anger, control, pride,
arrogance, self-pity, judgement, un-forgiveness.
He loves Me.
He comes to cleanse, forgive, release.

Me.
Loved, defended, protected, covered, belonging,
I look up to see an outstretched hand.
His.
"Shall we dance?"
Leading, listening, loving, knowing the way,
the steps, the music.

Him.
Nothing else matters. Nothing.
Just following
Him.
Only Him.
In the beauty, simplicity, and honesty of the dance.
Life, Living loved, authentic, abundant, free.
Him.

I hope today you are blessed, as we allow the Father to lead us in this beautiful dance of Grace.

Rain

The grass is dry and crunchy. It is not pleasant to walk across in bare feet. It doesn't mean to hurt; it's just not it's soft, supple self these days. I could stand for hours and water the grass, but it would be costly, all-consuming and still, in the end, not as good as rain.

There are large cracks in the earth. Gaping, waiting to be filled. Chasms, created because there is a lack. How is it that in the driest of times, weeds manage to thrive?

The garden looks good. It's because every other night I pull out the hose before I go to bed. I give it a good soaking to keep everything growing and living, but we are waiting.

We are waiting for rain, because nothing can really take its place. It will transform the garden and give the grass back its soft, green dress. It will erase the chasms, and new life will fill the thirsty, wilted stems and struggling blooms.

Our lives are often "dry and crunchy." We don't mean to be hurtful; it's just that sometimes we are not our supple, flexible selves. There are chasms in our lives that can't be filled;created because of lack. Not surprisingly, the enemy has a field day in these conditions! We can use the water we have to keep things alive, and looking OK on the surface, but it is costly, and all consuming. Nothing can really take the place of Living water. The deep down nourishing rain that the God of the universe is so good and willing to pour out on our spirits. It transforms our lives, makes things new, goes deep to the root and strengthens withered stems and blooms. It is life giving, refreshing and renewing!

I will pour water on thirsty ground and rain on dry land. I will pour my Spirit on your offspring and my blessing on your descendants. Isaiah 44.3 (GW)

Kitchen Talk

I love when a recipe comes with a story. Often when I am meandering through a used bookstore (read: little piece of heaven) I will look for old, worn, cookbooks. They usually have notes written in the margins, and I find them fascinating (I have never claimed to be without, um, quirks!) things like:

"Doubled this recipe to take to the Back River mission house. Leave out peppers for Mr. Abbot and hobo John."

I can't help it. My imagination goes into overdrive, and in short order I have a picture and story in my head to go with the hand scrawled notes. Even the inscriptions can tell a story.

"To Jenny on her 29th birthday, this should help you learn to cook. Love, Grandma Rose, December 1942".

See? Hands up if you didn't feel just a bit sorry for Jenny, and would have loved to have met Grandma Rose! There is something about preparing food and connecting in the kitchen that can bring about good stories and warm memories;

I was about 14 years old and standing beside my mom at the kitchen stove. She was making a lemon pudding. It was the good old fashioned kind that required cooking on the stove top, and lots of stirring. She had mixed in the water and was stirring the pale looking, cloudy liquid.

"It doesn't look like pudding." (Wasn't I an observant child?)

"I know, she said," but it will. Watch the middle of the pan. The hotter it gets the thicker and clearer it will get."

We stood, watching the rhythm of the stirring spoon. "Sometimes," she said "This is what happens in our lives, with God. We go through things that are hard, like the stirring and the heat, and we wonder why. He knows that in the end the cloudy places in us will be clear. Trust Him, when things get hard"

We watched as it slowly turned thick, clear and fragrant with lemony goodness! She poured the pudding into individual bowls, ready and waiting for dessert. I never forgot our kitchen talk!

I am reminded again that the God of the universe walks with us, lives in us, and is always longing to bring us into clear places of freedom, and all of us have a story.

What Are You Called?

I go by many names.
When I was young, I answered to "Kathy." When I went to college, the professors used my full name, "Katharine," and I didn't correct them. I like my full name, spelled with an "a" thank you!

Sometimes the things I have been called weren't so nice. To a teacher I was stupid, to a relentless group of boys in grades seven and eight I was ugly, fat and dumb. I have answered to "not good enough" "fearful" and "always wrong."

My mom used to call me darling, or sweetheart. Terms of endearment and ones that make me smile. My siblings call me Kath. To my nieces and nephews I am Auntie Kath, or Aunt Katharine.

If it's the school, the doctor, the dentist, etc... I am Mrs. Barrett. When one of my children calls me, it usually sounds like: Mum, mommy, momma, or mother (if they really need something). If I am lost at the computer in a piece of writing, and not responding they say "Hey Katharine!" To the best husband on the planet, I am Katharine, sweetie, hon, honey, baby, or hey gorgeous.

There is a point to all this! Over my cup of good coffee in a great mug, I have been thinking about this verse in Isaiah...

Do not be afraid, for I have ransomed you. I have called you by name; you are mine. When you go through deep waters, I will be with you. When you go through rivers of difficulty, you will not drown. For I am the Lord, your God... You are honored, and I love you. Isaiah 43.1-4 (NLT)

The God of the universe knows my name. My real name. I don't answer to any of the derogatory names anymore. They have been changed and they no longer define me. I know who I belong to, and it changes everything. He calls me:

Loved
Accepted
Beautiful
Daughter
Friend
Pure
Forgiven
Worthy
Precious
and many more!

His names for me are sweet to hear, and full of love and belonging. When He calls, I joyously answer to these.

What are you called?

The Swing at Dusk

I am not sure how long the bugs will let me stay. They have claimed the underside of the swing canopy as their place to celebrate the end of the day. A fading light party and I'm crashing it.

The birds and crickets have agreed to provide the music. Soft and almost hypnotic, it dares you to be caught up in the rhythm and still hold tight to stress or angst. I add to the melody with the steady creaking of the swing.

The sun has left, declining the party invitation. This soft, evening light reminds me of the glow of a night light. I remember my mom giving me one once, a long time ago, so I wouldn't be afraid. It makes me smile to think of the creator of the universe providing a night light. A comforting, caring, provision so that we are not plunged suddenly into darkness, so that we won't be afraid.

The bugs become a bit bolder in their attempt to bounce me from this venue. I wave my hands in half-hearted protest. If something so small can be so brave, then why not I?

I am not ready to leave. I still have half a cup of good coffee in a great mug, but I am not brave. I did not fight during the week when busy, sad, mundane, fear, apathy, and the tyranny of the urgent joined together and like a sponge, descended on my spirit. There was no courage then. But now, I am determined to talk and listen and be filled again, and to not allow another minute to go by without opening myself to the flooding of the one who gives me life.

Here, in the quiet safety of His night light. I flail my arms in a bold declaration of intention, and I wrap myself in the strains of twilight music. I belong. He never leaves. There is always Grace. No matter what the week may look like, He stays. He reminds me that I don't walk alone. We do this together.

It is dark now, but I am not afraid. My coffee cup is empty, but my spirit is effervescent. I have added grateful praise to the music of this night and even the sharp stab from the bravest of bugs cannot dampen it. I will leave them to their brave celebration, and I will rest in mine.

AUTUMN

For Tomorrow

The wind that whisks the leaves aloft
and streaks through tinted skies,
Is whispering in urgent tones,
filled with autumn sighs.

It calls across a field of orange
and begs for me to come.
It echoes in the baring trees
like haunting native drums.

It wraps around me like a cloak
of every color made,
Wanting to be recognized,
before the colors fade.

It wafts the scent of harvest
and the chill of shorter days.
It weaves in hollow spaces
where summer used to laze.

It beckons me to gather
'til I have had my fill,
To wander through the drying corn
and sumac studded hill.

It murmurs that it's leaving soon,
pushed on by frosted air.
And with it go the colors,
leaving all things bare.

But when the winter pall arrives,
and I am left with white,
I'll open up my memory
and savor Autumn's light.

Authentic

It's raining. My hair, which at the best of times has a mind entirely of its own, begins to droop. I don't mind. Not today. I am more concerned with not getting my new shoes wet. It's not because I care what she or anyone thinks of them, but because they are new, and suede, and I haven't yet sprayed them with protector. In perfect unison the wiper blades whisk off rain drops and speak in rhythm:

Au-then-tic, au-then-tic, au-then-tic, over and over like an anthem that echoes in my heart and begs to be heard. What does it mean to be authentic?

Real. Uncovered. As I was created. Unmasked. True to one's own spirit. Actual.

I am freshly washed skin and face. It has proven useless to cover it with any makeup on these days. Tears make short work of mascara and foundation. Does this count as Authentic?

I am early, she is late. I wait as she gets cereal, and while she eats, I talk. I recount the week's events. I have no good news; but no bad news either. Then she recalls the week and I listen. We laugh. Crystal clear laughter, that rings of friendship and honesty. She's in comfortable, not-yet-time for work clothes. She knows as well the futility of foundation and powder. Apologising for strewn toys around a comfy couch, she hears me say how much worse it would be if we were at my house. It is truth that the state of the living room makes no difference. Does it make this authentic?

And then we pray. This is why we set aside the morning. We never wanted to bring lists, to rhyme off points as if before a clerk, or judge. We want to sit with the creator. We want to know what His heart longs for. Our hearts long for truth, relationship, belonging. A holy dialogue with the God of the universe, here in this room and in every part of our walking and being. Real. Putting our hand in His and walking into the world with Him. Effective. Actual. Today, it feels like a list.

It is still raining when we say amen. The morning is finished, and yet I have one more thought, one question. So I ask.

"How are your mornings?"

Underneath the question, what I'm really saying, what is longing to be heard is this:

"My mornings aren't so good. I feel out of touch with the creator. I have let so many things crowd into my heart and time that the early morning peace and connections seem broken"

Her reply is honest, and her unmasking leaves room for me to uncover my own broken places. True spirits stand to face each other, and honesty steps forward to embrace them. This is real. Grace walks in from the rain, ready to be given and received. It's beautiful, and accompanied by Authenticity. They are woven together. Grace and Authentic follow me out the door and down the drive, wrapped around my shoulders like a cloak of fine fabric. Warm, and comforting, but as light and free as the leaves spinning from the nearly bare, wet maple tree.

My shoes are wet, and in need of a protector. My heart knows Grace, and the covering of Love.

It's a Tree!

When temperatures slip into the minus, I am glad for good, *hot* coffee in a great mug! The large windows in our living room, allow me a wonderful view of the neighborhood. In the yards all around us, the trees are shedding their leaves.

It is fascinating to me, that this process actually started back in August. When the days began to get shorter, the trees began a chemical change. They stopped growing, and all of the sap and resources for life, headed down to the root system. It will stay there, protected during the winter months, until it can safely head back upstairs to begin new growth in the spring. Amazing right?

While I was enjoying the sight of early morning sun and wind playing on those bare branches, I was marvelling at this thought:

It's a tree (deep, I know, but stay with me)

A tree that when it was created, was designed to accept life, produce and give life, and be protected and nourished. Down to the last detail! It is wired with intricate systems to keep it through all seasons.

And it's a tree.

If that much care and detail went into a tree, what about us?

A creator, so in love with what He has designed. So thrilled and delighted to wire us for His life, and Love and protection! So much more than anything He had created because we were designed for relationship with Him!

He holds every one of our moments, and if those moments are off kilter, broken or damaged, He knows what needs to be done. He has the original plans. And every one of them is covered by Grace.

It made me laugh out loud, for the sheer joy of being loved, protected and cared for more than I can begin to imagine! Whatever our days looks like, I hope they are full of moments of blessing and delight... knowing we are loved.

It's in the Everyday

He speaks. I know that well. Sometimes I forget to listen in the daily places.

Yesterday, it was windy. Crazy, sunny, make the tree branches sway windy! The laundry on the clothes line dried in no time. I was sitting on the swing, loving the wind, and watching the clothes blow on the line. The breeze caught my words and whisked them across the lawn.

"I wish it could be windy like this every laundry day!"

Grace for today. It echoed in my spirit, and I stopped the swing.

For today. I spread my hands on my lap and I list the graces of today that fill my heart and open my eyes to see Him here in;

Early Fall Sun, Wind that blows with wild abandon,

Enough clothes, A song most beautiful that plays in the top of the pine trees

Green tomatoes, still ripening on the vine.

Gratitude spills out onto the lawn. I repeat the Lord's Prayer because this line keeps coming back to me. "Give us this day our daily bread" Give us today what we need. For today. He is trustworthy and faithful. No grand chapel, lightning bolt or clever display. Just my laundry, the wind, and a God who speaks in the everyday. Speaking to me, to you. Reminding us that He is in the now. He is for us. Speaking. Listening. Loving.

Give your entire attention to what God is doing right now, and don't get worked up about what may or may not happen tomorrow. God will help you deal with whatever hard things come up when the time comes. Matthew 6:34 (MSG)

Forever and Always

Every one of his school days has started off like this: "Have a great day," I'd say. "Forever and always." He'd smile and call out, "Forever and always," as he walked down our front steps and headed off to school.

Every year as I watched him walk down the street, I marvelled at how quickly time had passed. Every year he grew taller, but it seemed like only yesterday he was a tiny seven pound baby. My youngest baby.

I don't know exactly when our exchange of "forever and always" started. I know that it was before he was able to reply. I would sing to him before bed, and as I turned out the light and closed the door, I would say, "I love you, forever and always." When he started talking he began to answer with "ever and alway" and soon it was a bedtime ritual.

I suppose, because he is my youngest, it was difficult for me when he started Kindergarten. (Oh let's be honest, I cried every time one of my four started kindergarten!) On the first day, when I hugged him and whispered, "Love you," he whispered back, "Forever and always." And the bed time ritual became the school time ritual as well.

Years slipped by, and he was walking to school on his own, staying for lunch, and learning to be responsible and independent. Every morning as he was leaving I reminded him that I loved him... forever and always, and he replied, "Love you... forever and always."

I hoped it was something that stayed with him during his day. A constant, in a world that can often be cold, confusing, and ever changing. As a parent, it delights my heart to hear him reply. It means he heard me, he's listening! I am glad for our relationship.

It seems no matter where my footsteps and thoughts take me, I always come back to Love. The love I have for my children often overwhelms me, but it cannot compare to the love our Heavenly Father has for us. He longs for relationship with us! For hearts that are always listening, hearing his voice saying, "I love you, forever and always, no matter what." His love never changes. It is the constant in my life. I am Loved. Living out of that love changes everything. It is the peace that allows us sweet sleep at night and the strength that helps us begin each uncertain day. It anchors the knowledge of who I am, and helps me discover who I was created to be. My reply to that love delights His heart (yes, He is thrilled and delighted by us!) "Love you... forever and always."

Why?

One Sunday afternoon we headed out to pick up a few groceries. That's when she flagged us down. We pulled over to the curb and she asked for directions to Lake Street. I pointed out the easiest route, she thanked us and then I rolled up my window. As she headed off down the street I turned to my husband.

"Maybe we should drive her, that's quite a walk."

We pulled up again, and offered her the lift.

"Yes, yes, thank-you. I live down by Lakeport and Ontario Street." The best husband offered, "My name is David." And I chimed in, "And mine's Katharine." She reached up to grasp my hand and said with a smile, "I'm Lorraine"

We apologised for the loud noise, our muffler had a hole in it and needed replacing. She said she didn't mind, that it was better than cold wind blowing in her face. I mentioned that it also looked like it might pour rain at any minute, and that is what prompted the story. Her story.

With slightly halting speech she explained why the rain always made her wish she were back in England where she was born. We heard about when she came here and how she hadn't been back in almost forty years. Full names, married and maiden. Full disclosure. Heritage, birth place, and longing.

And I wondered...Why?

Why are you walking such great distances? Why did you never get back to England? Why so trusting and eager to accept our offer? Why are the details so important to you? Details like where your father came from and exactly where you were born. Your thirteen year old devastation slips through in your words when you explain that you had to leave friends behind to come to a new country. The heart cry of needing to belong is louder than the muffler. All of the whys are answered somewhere in her story, and your story and mine.

We've all got one. Everything we do and say, the distances we walk in life and the ways we react, it all comes out of our story. All of the hours and days from before we first struggled to take a breath. All of the things that happened to us and around us and the life we live in reaction to those things.

Some of us keep the story to ourselves, never divulging any of it. We will ourselves to try and change our story or to figure out how to live within it. Others pour out the details to anyone who will listen, hoping that in doing so, the story will be changed. Some of us have lost pages, and spend long days trying to retrieve them.

We dropped her off at the corner of Lakeport and Ontario, and the wind snatched her "Thank you" and "God bless you" and swirled them down the street.

And this is grace: That He loves us, all of us, and knows the broken places in our stories. He came to heal them. To unwind the chains that lock us in the pages and keep us from walking in freedom.

And this is grace: The same spirit that welcomes me as I am, lives in me. He empowers me to offer grace to those I do not understand. To offer kindness instead of criticism, love instead of condemnation, acceptance instead of judgement. Not because I understand, or have it all together. Not out of pity, or self- importance, but because I too have my own "whys" and my own broken, wrinkled pages.

I have experienced the offering of grace poured out by those who were willing to look beyond the action, the reaction; to recognize that there must be a "why." They drew from that source of grace, to walk with me. It was a beautiful gift.

It started to rain as we drove away, and I whispered, "Grace and peace be with you, Lorraine." Often on a rainy day, I find myself looking for her when I drive to run my errands. I've never met her again, but I pray for her and her story. Each time I am overcome with gratitude for the opportunity to have given and received grace. It's beautiful.

Autumn Reflections

This particular time of year is my favorite! I love the warm days, and crisp cool evenings. There is a certain excitement in fields of golden corn stalks and watching flocks of birds head south. I love the pungent smell of fresh picked apples and the abundance of another harvest. I think that a field of pumpkins, waiting to be picked, is a breath-taking sight!

A light fragrant breeze reminds me that someone is already using their fireplace. Winter's icy grip is waiting just around the corner. The trees seem to be trying to outdo one another, each displaying a cloak of the finest red, orange, yellow and amber. So much that reminds us to be thankful.

Many years ago I was talking with some friends about how beautiful the fall colors were and how much I enjoyed them. A man standing nearby interrupted and said "It is just part of the process of preparing for winter. The only reason they change color is that they are dying." He was right.

The less chlorophyll, the more color. Those beautiful colors have actually been there all along we just couldn't see them for all the green.

That conversation always comes back to me when the leaves begin to change color. I think what that man meant to do, was to dampen our exuberance in something as simple as trees. What he did, was to remind me of the faithfulness of God in the seasons of our journey.

The reminder was this: No matter what I face or what season of the journey I might be in, there is always His life in me. When I feel most lacking, and when winter seems imminent, I am overwhelmed by His beauty, love and splendor. Perhaps if there were no autumns, we would miss this awesome facet of His life that is there all along, underneath the green.

I will take as many walks this Fall as I can. If I get the chance, I will jump in large piles of leaves, and choose pumpkins from a patch. I will join with family and friends in Thanksgiving for each other and for all we have been blessed with. Sometime during this season I will go walking where there are trees dressed in full Autumn colors. I will recall the faithfulness of God in the seasons of my journey, and in the hope of what lies ahead. Most of all, I want to rejoice in the awesomeness of the God of the universe, and His indescribable love for me no matter what the season! Join me?

Always Remember

I was hearing their conversation. It wasn't eavesdropping. They were just being and thinking, questioning in the living room before dinner. No formal platform or scheduled learning, just normal life talk, like breathing.

They are talking about the New Testament church, what it was, how it moved and breathed and how it was birthed. Who was there and why?

He is 14 years full of questions and curiosity, this son of mine. His heart is hungry and thirsty and open. He is not afraid to ask the why's and how's and who's. He wants to understand, to hear, to live, to learn.

He is 47 years full of questions and answers and experience, this husband of mine. His heart is hungry and thirsty, open and patient. He is full of passion for Him, The Creator, and for her, the Church. He is not afraid to ask and discuss and answer. He wants to listen, speak, share and learn.

Their words float around the room like stars on a clear night. They finish talking, and go back to reading, waiting for me to announce dinner. I'm still in the kitchen, standing on holy ground. This is what it should be, this is what it means:

Always remember these commands I give you today. Teach them to your children, and talk about them when you sit at home and walk along the road, when you lie down and when you get up. Write them down and tie them to your hands as a sign. Tie them on your forehead to remind you, and write them on your doors and gates. Deuteronomy 6.6-9 (NCV)

Sometimes and Always

Sometimes, it just is. Sometimes it is:
Busy days
Over cooked dinner that should have been fabulous
Long talks with teens
Moving in pre-determined motion without real feeling behind it
Fresh cooked dessert that no one liked
Lingering fears
Tired days
Unexpected rain falling on freshly hung laundry
Nights that don't quite erase the tiredness
Hearts wrung for the hard lessons our young ones often have to learn
Questions
Anxiety
Fog

Sometimes, it seems as if there are few choices for gratitude, but we find them. Even if it only begins with:

"Father, for today, thank-you that I know who I belong to."

And sometimes, we sit in the quiet of belonging, knowing that this is the best place to be, the only place our weighted feet are able to move to. The place that is safe.

And we offer up tomorrow. And trust Him. He doesn't just hold us, He holds everything.

Not just sometimes. ***Always.***

But I trust in your unfailing love; my heart rejoices in your salvation. Psalm 13:5 (NIV)

Walking with Angels through Iron Gates

Our son was about two at the time. I remember how my hands shook a little when I buckled him into his car seat. We were headed to the church Fall picnic, out at our Pastor's farm. I got into the driver's seat, buckled my seat belt, and just sat there. My husband was away for the weekend, at the wedding of a friend, and I was parenting alone for a few days. The salad (macaroni I think), lawn chairs and paraphernalia for the fab four were packed in the back. I was tired from a restless night of worrying.

He always did the driving.

The farm was about twenty minutes away, and there were two routes you could take: the old two lane highway or the main, four lane one. The latter wasn't even an option, not for me. But both of them terrified me. I didn't drive on the highway. I could run a household, and organize all kinds of events, and I managed to push through fear to do them, but I couldn't fight the driving fear. I drove in the city, to limited places. Safe, easy routes that I knew, and was comfortable with. Outside of those, I was gripped with paralyzing, numbing fear. And I told no one.

"Mommy! Let's go!"

I turned the key in the ignition, and put my head down on the steering wheel. The CD player whirred into action and music by Michael Card spilled onto the seats...

> *"Peter was locked up in prison,*
> *For the fearless faith he displayed.*
> *So God sent His angels to rescue,*
> *For that's what the brothers had prayed."*

"Please God," I prayed silently "Help me to do this"

> *"And so iron gates simply opened.*
> *His chains fell away like the sand.*
> *He reached out and followed his Guardian angel,*
> *Who led by invisible hands".*

My head jerked up and I clicked the back button, to listen to the words again. Meanwhile the kids were restless, and the clock was ticking."

> *"He sends His Angels,*
> *To open the prison doors.*
> *To come and set His captives free.*
> *To offer them more.*
> *To break open the doors of fear,*

Destroying dark dungeons of doubt.
He sends His angels to open the prison doors,
Lovingly they lead us out."

"Mommmeeeee!"

My head went back down on the steering wheel.

"Father, that's what I need. I need you to come and open doors for me. I can't do this." The little ones in the back seat calmed down, and I began to cry. Peace spilled out on the seats along with the music...

"So are you afraid of the darkness?
What's your personal prison today?
Ask Him to send you His angels,
So they might show you the way!"

"Father, I'm trusting you..."

Down the driveway, through the fear, and out on to the old highway. I just kept hitting the back button on the CD player until the farm came into view. On wobbly knees I set up our lawn chairs. I waited until most everyone had gone home before I left myself, so that it would be easy to drive out of the field. And I told no one. Not about the morning, the song, the prayer or the fear. What would they think of me? I hit the back button all the way home.

This was the beginning. I realized that freedom and healing might actually be possible. Years later, the God of the universe began to pinpoint roots of that fear, and I began walking through broken doors and finally leaving them behind!

One day, I even drove on the four lane! Not far, but far enough to make me smile. The only music I had was the sound of the wind and I may have heard the creaking of an iron gate! I still avoid the highway most of the time, and I still have far to go on this journey, but fear is no longer my constant companion. And I'm writing it down with fresh ink, because what you think of me doesn't matter. It's what He thinks of me. It's what you think of Him. He does amazing things.

"So are you afraid of the darkness?
What's your personal prison today?
Ask Him to send you His angels,
So they might show you the way!" (1)

I hope today finds you walking with angels, trusting the One who loves you immeasurably and is writing your beautiful story!

The day I call to you, my enemies will be turned back. I know this: God is on my side; the Lord, whose promises I praise. In him I trust, and I will not be afraid. Psalm 56: 9-11 (GNT)

(1) Card, Michael, "He Sends His Angels." <u>Close Your Eyes So You Can See</u>. Mole End Music (ASCAP), 1996.

Lifting My Head

It poured rain most of the weekend. At one point, the loud, lashing rain made the pastor raise his voice to be heard above the sound of the rain hitting the church roof! It was cold, wet and definitely a good weekend to stay indoors. Come evening, by the time my husband and I took the dog for a walk, the rain had stopped and all that was left were puddles.

I realized that I often walk with my head down, avoiding puddles, and focusing on the ground instead of what is up ahead. Too much downward gazing is causing me to miss out, and not just on our walks. I once said to someone, "Don't look where you are, look to where you are going. It changes how you walk (or run or skate). Too much focus on the ground in front of you makes your progress slow, your steps faltering and you miss so much!" I needed to take my own advice.

Discouragement, the need to avoid possible puddles, and focusing on the immediate had left me walking slow, head down and not really seeing or listening to anything else except what was right in front of me. I had been listening to some very old whispers that swirled upward, telling me I was not smart enough or worthy of some of the good things that I had been waiting for, and walking towards.

But then He comes. When I am standing in those puddles, the God of the universe is there to be my shield. And when my King lifts my head, I can hear on the breeze the voice of the Spirit. It banishes the whisper of lies and replaces them with truth. I take a step in honor, and another in courage. Ahead, there is light and life.

But You, O LORD, are a shield about me, my glory, and the One who lifts my head. Psalm 3:3 (NASB)

I am so thankful to walk with the God who gently lifts my head. I want to focus on where He is leading. I want to keep discovering who I was created to be...I don't want to miss a thing!

Daughters

Beautiful, radiant, priceless gifts, entrusted to us for a little while.
Kind, Sensitive, Spirited.
Fun-loving, Passionate, Curious, Loving.
Generous, and Compassionate.

They are so loved. Not for what they do, but for who they are. Young women, discovering who they were created to be. Listening for the Father's heart, His calling and direction. They bring us more laughter, love and joy, than we ever thought possible.

No matter how many years pass, sometimes when they smile, we can only see the tiny babe that took hold of our hearts and never let go. Or the two year old, with the impish grin and a pocket full of dirt.

It started way back then. With every turn of the road and new adventure, I've heard the whisper. It reminds me to open my heart, my hands. Loosen my grasp and step back. I have been slowly letting go. It's what this whole process has been about.

Holding them close, covering them, protecting them, giving them room, backing off, praying, loving and watching them to be able to stand, walk, run and fly.

I think they have taught us far more than we have taught them. We are still learning.

A Blessing for Daughters:

We bless the sweet, amazing, wonderful gift of you. That God decided to make you a daughter, unique, like no one else on earth. May you be blessed to understand the plans God has for you, to hear His spirit and see the world, the church, as He does. May you continue to discover this amazing identity that is yours alone, and hand in hand with the God of the universe, walk into all that you were created for! You are loved, cherished, and delighted in! We are blessed, because you are our daughter.

Grapes and Grace

I don't do a lot of canning or preserving, but of the things I do, I love making grape juice the best. Maybe it's because it starts with beautiful globes of sweetness. Or maybe it's because I go to the farmer's market to get the bushel of grapes, and I love the market!

The smell that fills the house while they cook is, I think, one of the loveliest scents of Fall! Steamy grape goodness wafts down the stairs and even from the front door, it's evident that juice is being made! Once the juice is all cooked off, all that is left is a large pile of skins and stems. Gross as it looks, there is still something wonderful tucked inside this mess. I leave it to drain overnight and the slightly thicker juice that fills the pan is what I use to make jelly.

I stood stirring the jelly before I jarred it, and I couldn't help but embrace hope. If the God of the universe could provide amazing syrup from the mess of steamed stems and skins...He would make something beautiful from the messy circumstances in our lives. If you look at the pile of broken-down grapes, you ONLY see a mess. They have been steamed and squished and piled in a colander! Overnight though, while it rests, sweet juice flows out, and it makes the most amazing tasting jelly!

Beautiful right?

I know I am not alone in sometimes feeling steamed and squished and piled in the discard pile. But redeemed can look like jars of deep purple jelly, beautiful, fragrant, and sweet. He is good, He does good work, and this is what He says...

I will make rivers flow on the dry hills and springs flow through the valleys. I will change the desert into a lake of water and the dry land into fountains of water....The desert and dry land will become happy; the desert will be glad and will produce flowers. Like a flower, it will have many blooms. It will show its happiness, as if it were shouting with joy. It will be beautiful. Isaiah 41:18, 35:1,2 (NCV)

Lined up in finished rows on the counter, they stood ready. Rows of reminders, sentinels to the cold winter days ahead!

GRACE AND FRESH INK

WINTER

A Cup of Quiet

It is a quieter time,
Lulled to sleep by longer days and deeper skies.
The season settles in.
Twigs snap, ice cracks, and winds slice hard
through bare fields.
Shivering, nature wraps herself in exquisite
blankets of white,
And sends her little ones to sleep.
Candles flicker and chimney smoke rises.
Wool and down become the choice of those who
brave the breath-stealing breezes.
Beyond the quiet, beneath the white is the sound.
Steady and rhythmic
The deepest of frosts and the thickest of snows
will not extinguish it.
It is the sound of Hope, of waiting.
It is the unseen miracle of Winter.
The secret green beneath the white.
It's life,
and it slumbers, safe in Winter's depths.
Bright sun glints off snowy hills.

Seasons cycle, and the creator calls.
Winter smiles, and drinks a cup of quiet.

Letting in the Light

It may be -14 degrees Celsius, but I really don't mind when the sun is shining brilliantly! I need light, especially in the darker winter months. I take extra vitamin D to try and make up for shorter days, but nothing is as good as the sun. This morning, I went around and opened all the blinds to let in the light, and as I did, I thought about this:

When I opened the blinds, the sun illuminated the dust on my coffee table... (Yes, dust. It happens, often.) It was on the lower shelves, and until the sun shone on it, I didn't notice it. I got out the furniture polish, and whisked it away (doing a "happy the sun's out" dance, I might add).

How sad it would be if I never opened the blinds, just relied on the vitamin D!

I know sometimes that is what I do with the God of the universe. I keep the blinds shut. I try and find other things to make up for lack of light, and work on the dusting myself. I do the best I can, with what I have.

I know that if I open the doors/blinds to some parts of my life, he will flood it with His light. And if there's dust, He is amazing at whisking it away! It is so much better than if I try to do it myself. I also know the great delight of having Him join me in the "sun's out" happy dance! In His light, there is peace, joy, healing and unending love!

Winter days aren't always my favorite, but I do enjoy basking in the light that pours through my windows, and the Light that floods my Spirit!

Happy Dance anyone?

For with you is the fountain of life; in your light we see light. Psalm 36:9 (NIV)

Drumming and Belonging

His hands easily cover mine now, but I remember. I recall small, sweet toddler hands that tapped on pots, tables, toys. Keeping time with the music on the stereo, the car radio or the notes in his head. It never stopped. Sometimes I reach over and attempt to cover his gentle hands with mine, and he smiles. I need the break, but he never does. It's in him. It's part of who he is. It's beautiful.

We walk into the cafe and find seats easily. Later, it will fill to capacity and I love the feeling of music swirling around a packed Friday night crowd. He is part of the opener. His first acoustic gig. Hands on drum, heart pouring out through his fingertips.

My son.

My heart swells beyond where I think it can safely go and my throat constricts with the opening song. I'm proud of him. I love watching him learn who he was created to be. I enjoy a mug of good coffee and pour out thanks to the one who created him.

I smile when I catch his eye, and put my hands together at the end of each song. When he comes back to the table we tell him how good it was, and remind him again how glad we are that he is ours. We order Chai tea and listen to the next set.

I let the music be the background for my thoughts... I wonder if this is anything like the way He feels - the God of the universe - when we're walking this journey, and we're learning the truth of who we were created to be. When we walk for a moment living loved, does He elbow an angel and say, "That's my daughter!"

I smile between sips, because I know that He is always reminding me that I belong to Him, that I'm loved. It's personal. It is real. It's relational. He *loves* watching; healing and helping me uncover who I was created to be. It's His heart, and has been from the moment He saw all of me in only a spark of light. Beautiful.

Cold air catches my breath as we leave the cafe. Snow crunches under foot and stars create a canopy overhead. His tapping on the van seat, breaks the silence and I smile..."That's my son!"

I Get It!

On Sunday morning there were five candles at the front of the church, one was lit. Advent Candles.

I spent a few minutes of the service lost in the memory of Advent in years past. I missed participating in the candle lighting each week. The new church does things differently. I let the names and faces of those I had done Advent with over the years float past my mind's eye and I prayed for them, blessed them, wherever they were for Advent.

In all of my pondering, I was caught by this thought that will not let go. Immanuel, God with us. With us. Maybe it is because of the places I have walked in my journey lately, that make this thought so captivating, enveloping and real. God with us, in us. Immanuel.

> There is Hope, because He is Hope
> and He is with us.
> There is Joy, because He is Joy
> and He is with us.

> There is Peace, because He is Peace
> and He is with us.

He is with us in the beautiful, the good. In the sorrow, lies, and truth. Present in the expected, the unexpected and the loss. Speaking, listening, loving - with us.

It takes my breath away, and pulls me close into a safe, warm place. It opens my eyes and ears and lets me walk in places I would never have gone, speaking with a voice I would never have dared to use. It allows me to reach out beyond myself because,

> I. am. never. alone.
> Immanuel - God with us.

There have been many Advent seasons, but this one is different. The same, beautiful message rings out in familiar tones, but this year, I get it. It fills me with pure delight and I know that the God who is with me, that lives in me, is delighted as well!

Behold, the virgin shall be with child, and shall bring forth a son, And they shall call his name Immanuel; which is, being interpreted, God with us. Matthew 1:23 (KJV)

Weary

Sometimes, at the end of a day, a week, a month, I am Weary...

wea•ry ; adj. wea•ri•er, wea•ri•est Weary in (Body)....1. Physically or mentally fatigued (Soul). 2. Expressive of or prompted by fatigue: a weary smile. (Spirit)...3. Having one's interest, forbearance, or indulgence worn out: weary of delays. 4. Causing fatigue; tiresome: a weary wait.

I need to stop, to listen...

I am quick to convince myself that I am the one who fixes things, who takes control, who may have the answers. My feet begin to root in soil that is not organic to me. I look for quick answers in the closest places and the things I choose make things heavier and slower and my feet sink deeper into terra firma.

I try and sleep more, choose my activities wisely, prioritize. I give more; I step back and allow others in front. I read and pray with purpose and plan and take on more good responsibilities. And it leaves me even more...Weary.

So I stop, if only to try and regroup and reposition. And then I hear it. It is a voice that echoes in the deep places within me. Places soaked with Grace. It tells me that I have forgotten.

The impact of His voice in the midst of my chaos, reminds me of the glass-like stillness of a lake at dawn. I stand completely still, so as not to disturb anything. And I listen.

Come to me, all you who are weary and burdened, and I will give you rest. Take my yoke upon you and learn from me, for I am gentle and humble in heart, and you will find rest for your souls. For my yoke is easy and my burden is light. Matthew 11:28-30 (NIV)

I remember. I remember where my help comes from. I am reminded, who it is that holds all things in His hands, and gives me life. I know where I need to go. I am reminded that I was created for so much more, and that another home awaits me. I slowly exhale, and I suddenly realize, I've been holding my breath.

What's on Your List?

She was so sweet. She was sitting on the floor in the middle of a store. The best husband and I were meandering down the main aisle finishing up our Christmas shopping. This little girl with dark brown hair and big brown eyes was sitting on top of a box almost as big as she was. She slid down the side, but her hands never left the box. When we stopped at the end of a row, I watched her sit on the floor, little hands still clutching the box, staring at the label... it looked like a doll house. Her family was moving on to another section, but she wasn't going anywhere! We smiled, and the best husband said "Well, I guess she knows what she wants."

It is the season for lists. We asked our children to make us a list, and we are delighting in finding a gift for them that is something we know they would love. Socks and underwear can wait for another day, I want to get them something that reflects who they are, who they were created to be. It is different for each of them. We can't always get what's on the list, but sometimes, we find something even better!

Driving home from the mall, I had this thought; what's on my list? Not the perfume, slippers, etc. list. I mean the list that my heart and spirit carry. The deep down desires of my heart. The ones that start as dreams, hopes and nudges from the God of the universe. While I watched the Christmas lights flit past the car window, something in my spirit whispered, "Don't let go. Ask Him again, for the thing that your heart desires."

We have been showered with gifts: adoption, redemption, forgiveness. He is constantly lavishing on us grace upon grace. He knows exactly what we were created to be, and what He gives and where He leads will reflect that, and Him.

Maybe today, we can take out that heart list. If the ink has faded, let's write again in bold strokes. We can, because we are His children. He wants us to ask. We may not get exactly what's on the list, it may be something better, but whatever He does is good! Whatever your heart dreams of today, don't let go, ask Him again!

Delight yourself in the LORD; And He will give you the desires of your heart. Commit your way to the LORD, Trust also in Him, and He will do it. Psalm 37:4,5 (NASB)

The Big Picture

Remember those "guess what it is" books? They would show you a small, close-up photo of an object, and you tried to guess what the full picture was. Our children loved to try and guess what the object was and spent many hours poring over those types of books at the library.

Yesterday I was thinking about this journey I'm on and what it looks like. (Nothing serious. Just a few thoughtful moments in the morning and some mulling in the shower before dinner.) There are some times in life that I wish I could see the big picture, not just the small part of it that I find myself in, at this moment in time.

Sometimes it seems obvious and other times I am lost in the detail and not sure what this time might mean in the grand scheme of things. My aha! moment was this: If I thought I knew what the big picture was, and where this part of my journey was headed, I would probably try and manipulate things so that I would end up where I thought I should be. Soap bubbles swirled, while I considered that I would probably trust less and control more. I have just started learning what it means to bask in the freedom of letting go and trusting God with all of my life and its beautiful mess. So I put down the soap, and set down my "need to know."

There is much less worry when I remember who I trust, and focus on the "now" part of this journey. It is wonderful, crazy, authentic, difficult, and breath-taking, and I am not in charge!

The LORD is my strength and my shield; my heart trusts in him, and he helps me. My heart leaps for joy, and with my song I praise him. Psalm 28:7 (NIV)

Hark the Herald Angels

I remember exactly where I was. I remember the crowd of people, everyone's voices raised. When we came to my favorite carol, I sang loud and long, and then, at one phrase, I stopped. Everyone was still singing, but it seemed to grow quiet as I repeated the phrase. It was as if I was hearing it for the first time.

> *"Born to raise the sons of earth,*
> *Born to give them second birth"*

I am a daughter of this earth. That makes me His daughter and it makes Him my Father. I never finished singing the carols. Tears streamed down my face, as something that I had heard and sung a thousand times before, now settled in my spirit and became real. I was seventeen. I knew the God of the universe as my own, and by many names: Savior, Protector, God, and King... but now, Father. I was a daughter of the King! A King with authority over everything in heaven and on earth, and He was pleased to dwell with me. Emmanuel, God with us.

Since that day in the crowd, I have learned a lot about what it means to be a daughter of the King, to have a real, intimate relationship with the God of the universe. I still have a lot to learn. I let things stand in the way of our relationship, and often need reminders of who I am. It is still a journey of discovery and Grace. Probably the most important thing that I am just beginning to grasp... How very much my Heavenly Father loves me, and what it means to live out of that love.

Hail the heaven-born Prince of Peace!
Hail the Son of Righteousness!
Light and life to all He brings
Risen with healing in His wings.
Mild He lays His glory by
Born that man no more may die.
Born to raise the sons of earth
Born to give them second birth.
Hark! The herald angels sing,
"Glory to the newborn King!"

This is the joy of Christmas. I will join the triumph of the skies! I will sing at the top of my lungs: He is Peace and Healing and Light and Life! Born to raise me! A most magnificent Dad. Trustworthy, unwavering and true. I belong to Him. His life is in me. Born to earth because of unfathomable, unconditional, all-encompassing Love!

The Stone of Help

I was going through some boxes to find a photograph I needed. My pictures are just not that organized, so I had to sift through many photos to find what I wanted. With every envelope I opened I kept repeating the same thing:

"Oh, I remember that," or, "Oh, I had forgotten that!" In the middle of the reminiscing, this verse dropped into my heart.

"The reason I can still find hope is that I keep this one thing in mind: the Lord's mercy...His compassion is never limited. It is new every morning. His faithfulness is great." Lamentations 3.21-23 (GW)

Lamentations is not the first place you would think to go in order to find an encouraging verse!

It was a time in our lives when we had so many questions. We were looking for answers and encouragement in a shaky and fearful time. I stopped my photo search to read the verse and listen for the heart of the God of the universe.

It was one part of our lives, one chapter in our book. If we look back, flipping through pages of our story, we do a lot of "Oh I remember that," and, "Oh, I had forgotten that!" There are snapshots of our days, reminders of when God has walked with us, stood for us, and held us. They are reminders that He is still doing those things. He has no limit. He has been faithful and promises to keep being faithful.

In 1Samuel there is the story of God walking with His people in a battle. When they won, Samuel took a large stone and placed it between two cities and called it Ebenezer (It means "the stone of help"). He placed it there as a reminder that up to that point in their journey, God had helped them. It wasn't always a pretty story. There was winning, losing, confusion, and peace. But God was there, on every page.

Sitting in the midst of boxes and photos, I set up an Ebenezer that day. I wanted to mark that place. God had been faithful in every part of my story up to that day. I knew He would keep helping, walking, standing and holding, in all my tomorrows. Setting up the stone meant that I would trust Him with the next line, page, and chapter, no matter what they might look like.

I hope your day is filled with moments of remembering faithfulness.

A New Year

Years ago when our children were very small, we had a very memorable New Year's Eve. My in-laws were staying with us and graciously offered to watch our children while we went out for dinner. On the drive home, it began to snow. It was that soft, quiet snow that blankets everything, and changes the world into a sparkling beautiful place, even if only for a few hours.

It wasn't quite midnight, so we didn't want to go in the house yet. Instead, we decided to go for a walk. Hand in hand in falling snow, we walked to the tiny cafe on the corner. It was the perfect place to stop for coffee.

The very pregnant hostess smiled and invited us in. There were only a handful of people, and later we apologised for being the only ones that weren't family, but they greeted us warmly and offered us something to drink. Sitting in front of the window watching the snow, we talked about the coming year, our hopes and dreams. Music played, laughter rang out from the kitchen. As midnight approached, the owner propped open the front door with a brick. Cold air swirled around our feet. Turning to us, she explained:

"It's our custom. We open the door to let the old year out, and celebrate the arrival of the new one."

She rubbed the top of her baby-full belly and smiled. The arrival of the New Year would usher in the arrival of their daughter. Many times that year we would pass on the street, each of us with a child in a stroller.

Midnight brought a rush of well wishes, a kiss from the best husband, and then we left them to finish their celebrations. I remember how warm and full it felt. How good to spend the start of the new year in that place, even though we were strangers. We left our footprints in fresh snow, as we began walking into a new year.

There have been many years since then, when I have propped open the door. Some years I have been more anxious than others to see it leave!

Our celebrations have changed as family has grown. We talk, laugh, and watch fireworks. At some point near midnight, I usually prop open the door and the cold air that swirls around my feet reminds me that the old year is leaving. The New Year is always unknown, but I can be full of peace, hope and anticipation. I do not know where our footsteps will take us, but I know, perhaps more

GRACE AND FRESH INK

with each year's passing, that we do not walk alone. He is and always will be, Emmanuel, God with us.

As we approach a New Year, may you be blessed with knowing more of who God is, and who you are to Him.

Otters and Love

The tree is bare, and so are the walls. It feels good to have things clean and clear again! It's time to slowly move into life in a New Year. We have a tradition of leaving our opened gifts and stockings under the tree after Christmas. Yesterday I was sending gifts to appropriate rooms, and remembering how delighted they were with this or that. Thanks to a phenomenally good sale, the best husband received a Blackberry Play book from the kids and me on Christmas morning.

At least once a day we have heard him comment on how much: he loves it, he likes it, and it's awesome! It will be a great tool for him at home and at school. After Christmas, he went online and ordered an Otter box (I speak as if I am knowledgeable on these things... I'm not, but I'm learning!)

It's a case that protects the playbook. It's built so that if the tablet falls, the Otter box protects the screen from hitting the floor, and absorbs the shock. It has a screen protector as well, so that all the "touch" on the touch screen won't go too deep and cause permanent damage.

I can feel your eyes glazing over! Wait, stay with me, there is a thought that emerged in the middle of all this! This morning I was reading this:

I love you, Lord. You are my strength. The Lord is my rock, my protection, my Savior. My God is my rock. I can run to him for safety. He is my shield and my saving strength, my defender. Psalm 18:1,2 (NCV)

My Otter Box! Then I turned to this (One of my favorite places)

Those who go to God Most High for safety will be protected by the Almighty. I will say to the Lord, "You are my place of safety and protection. You are my God and I trust you." Psalm 91:1,2 (NCV)

No matter where I may find myself, He is there. My protector. He will help with the shock when I fall. The things that push against me, arrows that try and go deep, they hurt, but God says that they don't have to cause permanent damage. He will be my shield.

Of course! He loves us, is delighted with us. He is for us, and with us. He wants to protect and cover us because that's what you do for something that belongs to you!

There are twelve new months laid out before us. They wait for new footprints on uncharted, unknown paths. Our hearts can be content knowing who we belong to and who covers us! May it be a year of peace, light, truth and deep joy. May every footstep you take, echo this truth:

You are loved wildly, unconditionally and completely by the God of the universe, and He is delighted with you!

Beautiful Refuge

Snow days! Sometimes I think that snow days are one of my favorite parts of winter! I love getting up at 6:00am, checking the news report, and then slipping back under a still -warm duvet to catch a few more hours of sleep!

On our last snow day, I stood in front of the window at 6:00am, and watched the snow from a darkened living room. The wind was whipping snow from the roof and tossing it in cold, icy, drifts around the door and I was dry and safe. Our house can withstand the winds, and I was glad for a furnace that works well at keeping us warm!

In the warm shelter of the early morning, this verse kept replaying in my mind:

Those who live in the shelter of the Most High will find rest in the shadow of the Almighty. This I declare about the Lord: He alone is my refuge, my place of safety; he is my God, and I trust him. Psalm 91.1,2 (NLT)

However loudly life howls around the door and threatens our safety, warmth, our place...I am so glad I can trust Him. My refuge. The One I run to, live in and rest with.

Whatever the storms are today, whatever rages. No matter how strong or how high it drifts at the door. There is one who is stronger and in His beautiful refuge there is no fear, only Peace.

Whatever the weather you find yourself in today, I hope you are in His refuge, full of warmth, beauty and peace!

Waiting for Spring

Today as I was walking to work, I noticed it. Not a lot of it, but enough to make me stop for a moment to savor it: blades of grass! The warm, brilliant sun and milder temperatures have melted the snow, in some places right down to the grass.

Most of it is brown and straggly, but grass none the less! I stood staring at the snow, wanting it to be gone, all of it in one fell swoop. Not only that, but I really wanted it to be spring, all at once. I imagined turning a full 360 degree circle on the side walk and having it become fully spring by the time I reached the end of the spin. Sort of like the Narnia movie, when Aslan breathes, and winter leaves!

While I waited at a stop light, I starred at the grass, and this is what my heart heard.

"You can stare at the grass and wish away the snow, but only the God of the universe calls the seasons and sets the time in motion."

All of this pondering had more to do with my own life than with spring's arrival, but it was a good picture for me. Hope doesn't come from staring at the grass, or even the small signs of spring. Hope is from the one who holds all of my moments and days. The One who knows every part of me, and loves me, completely. I may not understand why some things (like freedom and healing) don't come all in one fell swoop, but I think that standing and staring doesn't help.

I walk despite the ice and snow, because some of it has melted, and I am able to walk where I couldn't before. The shift in temperature has slowly melted the huge icicles that were hanging from the roof. I didn't even realize that they had fallen off until I looked out the kitchen window and I could see clearly to the road!

I am so thankful for the new places in my life that I now walk in freely. Things continue to fall away and I have sight that I didn't have before. Aslan is breathing, in His time. So many things have changed, but not because I wished or willed them to. I can't make grass grow, I'm not in charge. I can turn my focus to the One who is in charge, and delight in the warmth of the sun and the freedom to pull off my gloves and feel the breeze. I trust Him. He promised to complete the good work that He started.

For I am confident of this very thing, that He who began a good work in you will perfect it until the day of Christ Jesus. Philippians 1:6 (NASB)

~ About The Author ~

Katharine makes her home in Ontario, Canada where she shares life, and laughter with her husband and four children. She is on a journey with the God of the universe, discovering who she was created to be, and what it means to walk living loved, in everyday grace. <u>***Grace and Fresh Ink***</u> is Katharine's first book. Most days you can find her blogging through life, love, laughter, creativity, family and faith, at ***Just A Thought***, always listening for His heart and never without a cup of good coffee in a great mug!

You can find out more about Katharine at:

http://www.katharinesthoughts.net

Follow her on Twitter:@kathsthoughts
and
Facebook:
http://www.facebook.com/katharinesthoughts
or visit
http://www.graceandfreshink.com

www.ingramcontent.com/pod-product-compliance
Lightning Source LLC
Chambersburg PA
CBHW071511040426
42444CB00008B/1596